P9-BYY-982

NBA CHAMPIONS

OKLAHOMA CITY THUNDER

AARON FRISCH

CREATIVE EDUCATION

Published by Creative Education
P.O. Box 227, Mankato, Minnesota 56002
Creative Education is an imprint of The Creative Company
www.thecreativecompany.us

Book and cover design by Blue Design (www.bluedes.com)
Art direction by Rita Marshall
Printed by Corporate Graphics in the United States of
America

Photographs by Getty Images (Andrew D. Bernstein/NBAE,
Tim Defrisco, Ron Hoskins/NBAE, Walter Iooss Jr./NBAE,
George Long/Sports Illustrated, George Long/WireImage,
Melissa Majchrzak/NBAE, Layne Murdoch/NBAE, Joe
Murphy/NBAE, NBA Photo Library/NBAE, Mike Powell, Dick
Raphael/NBAE, Larry W. Smith/NBAE, Rocky Widner/NBAE,
Jeremy Woodhouse)

Library of Congress Cataloging-in-Publication Data

Frisch, Aaron.
Oklahoma City Thunder / by Aaron Frisch.
Includes index.
Summary: A basic introduction to the Oklahoma City
Thunder professional basketball team, including its
formation as the Seattle SuperSonics in 1967, greatest
players, championship, and stars of today.
ISBN 978-1-60818-144-5
1. Oklahoma City Thunder (Basketball team)—History—
Juvenile literature. I. Title.
GV885.52.O37F75 2012
796.323'640976638—dc22   2010051577

CPSIA: 030111 PO1448

First edition
9 8 7 6 5 4 3 2 1

3 1907 00312 9722

Cover: Kevin Durant
Page 2: Russell Westbrook
Right: Kevin Durant (with ball)
Page 6: Jeff Green

TABLE OF CONTENTS

The Thunder's mascot is a bison named Rumble

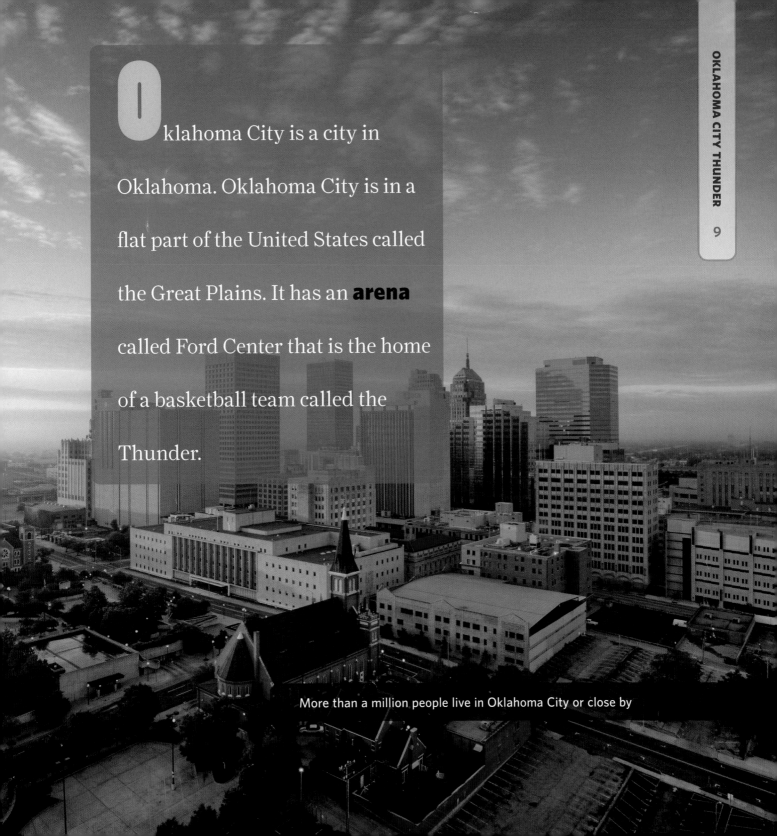

Oklahoma City is a city in Oklahoma. Oklahoma City is in a flat part of the United States called the Great Plains. It has an **arena** called Ford Center that is the home of a basketball team called the Thunder.

More than a million people live in Oklahoma City or close by

Lenny Wilkens

The Thunder are part of the National Basketball Association (NBA). All the teams in the NBA try to win the **NBA Finals** to become world champions. The Thunder play many games against teams called the Jazz, Nuggets, Timberwolves, and Trail Blazers.

The Thunder started playing in 1967. They played in Seattle, Washington, then and were called the SuperSonics. Lenny Wilkens was one of Seattle's first great players. He was a guard who also coached the team.

In 1978, the SuperSonics got to
the NBA Finals. They lost to the
Washington Bullets, but the next
year, center Jack Sikma helped them
get back to the Finals. This time they
beat the Bullets to become world
champions!

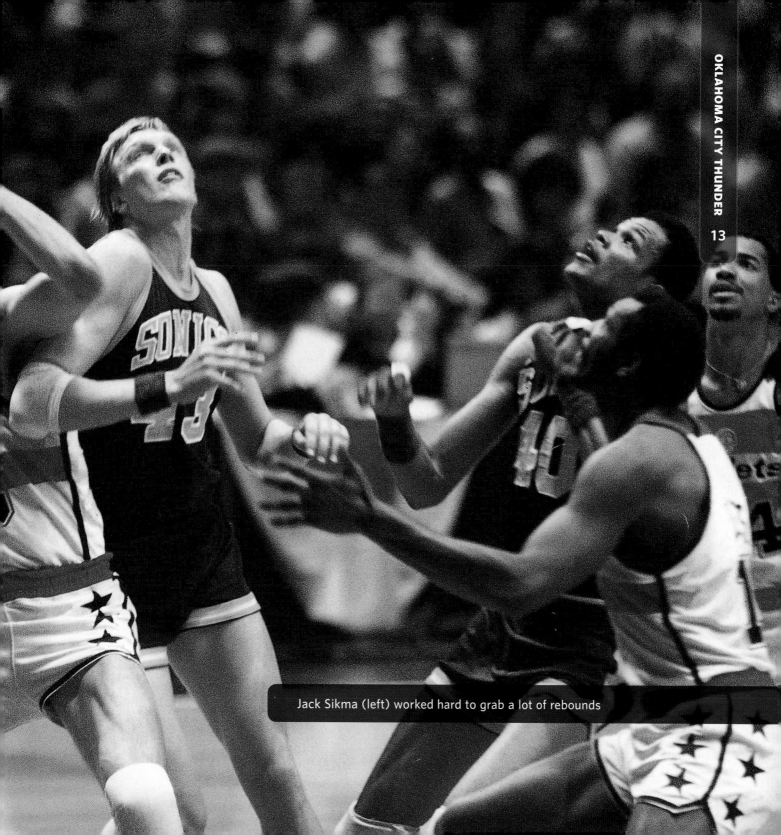

Jack Sikma (left) worked hard to grab a lot of rebounds

Slick Watts was a quick guard for Seattle in the 1970s

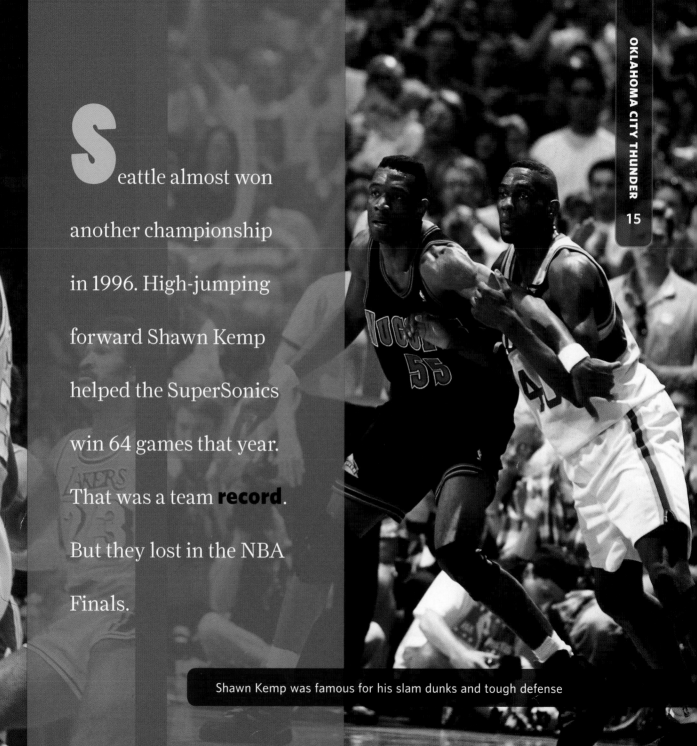

Seattle almost won another championship in 1996. High-jumping forward Shawn Kemp helped the SuperSonics win 64 games that year. That was a team **record**. But they lost in the NBA Finals.

Shawn Kemp was famous for his slam dunks and tough defense

THUNDER FACTS

- Started playing: 1967 (as the Seattle SuperSonics)

- Conference/division: Western Conference, Northwest Division

- Team colors: blue, orange, yellow, and white

- NBA championship:

  1979 — 4 games to 1 versus Washington Bullets

- NBA Web site for kids: http://www.nba.com/kids/

Seattle was not as good after that. In 2008, the SuperSonics' owner moved the team to Oklahoma City. The team changed its name to the Thunder and got new uniform colors.

The Thunder became Oklahoma City's first big sports team

SuperSonics stars Xavier McDaniel (above) and Fred Brown (opposite)

The SuperSonics had many stars. Guard Fred Brown was a team **captain** who loved to shoot three-pointers. Forward Xavier McDaniel was a tough rebounder nicknamed "The X-Man."

SAY IT LIKE THIS

Xavier
ZAY-vyer

Seattle fans nicknamed Nate McMillan "Mr. Sonic"

Nate McMillan joined Seattle in 1986. He was a guard who played for the SuperSonics all 12 seasons of his **career**. Gary Payton was another great guard. Fans called him "The Glove" because he played such tight defense.

Gary Payton played tough defense but was a slick passer, too

In 2007, the SuperSonics added fast forward Kevin Durant. He averaged more than 30 points per game in his third season! Oklahoma fans hoped that he would help lead the Thunder to their first NBA championship in Oklahoma City!

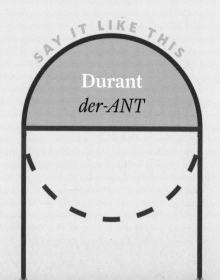

SAY IT LIKE THIS

Durant
der-ANT

By 2011, Kevin Durant was one of the biggest stars in the NBA

GLOSSARY

arena — a large building for indoor sports events; it has many seats for fans

captain — a player who is the main leader on a team besides the coach

career — all of the seasons that a person plays

NBA Finals — a series of games between two teams at the end of the playoffs; the first team to win four games is the champion

record — something that is the most or best ever

INDEX